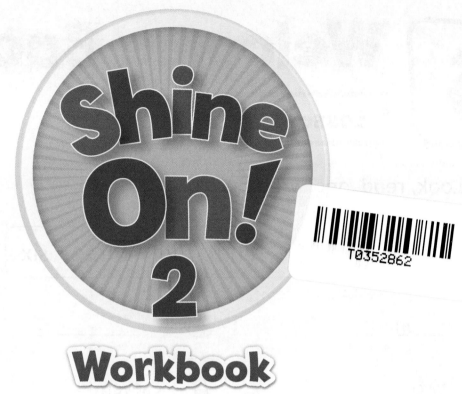

Contents

OXFORD
UNIVERSITY PRESS

Welcome Back!

Lessons 1 and 2

1 Look, read, and write.

~~one~~ nine five three six

1 _one_

2 two

3 _____

4 four

5 _____

6 _____

7 seven

8 eight

9 _____

10 ten

2 Look, read, and match. Say the letters.

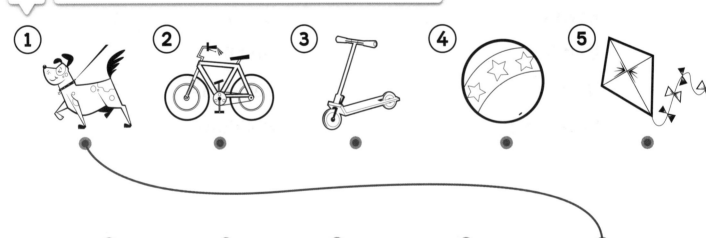

① ② ③ ④ ⑤

bike ball kite scooter dog

1 Look, read, and match.

①

②

● sad

● goodbye

● happy

③

● hello

④

Happy Birthday!

1 Look, read, and make a ✓ or an ✗.

①

clown   ✓

balloon   ✗

②

candle ☐

present ☐

③

cake ☐

card ☐

④

balloon ☐

card ☐

⑤

cake ☐

present ☐

⑥

candle ☐

clown ☐

4   **Vocabulary** balloon, clown, candle, present, card, cake

1 Count, read, and match.

① 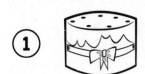 ●

②  ●

③ ● (candles)

④ ● (dice)

⑤ ● (balloons)

⑥ 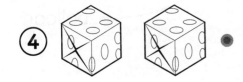 ●

● 2 presents

● 1 present

● 4 cards

● 9 cards

● 3 clowns

● 6 clowns

● 1 cake

● 2 cakes

● 4 candles

● 7 candles

● 8 balloons

● 5 balloons

Grammar There's a cake. There are seven cakes.

1 What's missing? Match.

①

②

- basketball

- Megabyte

③

- balloon

- cake

④

2 Read, look, and circle.

1 puzzle

2 car

3 basketball

4 robot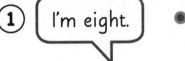

Everyday English!

3 Look, read, and match.

How old are you?

① 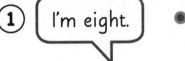 I'm eight.   •

② I'm six.   •

③ I'm three.   •

④ Me, too!   •

1 Are the sides the same or different? Look and circle.

①

(the same) / different

②

the same / different

③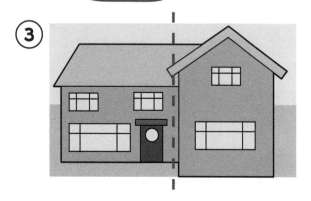

the same / different

④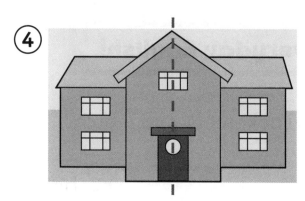

the same / different

2 Draw. Make the sides the same.

1 Look, read, and count. Write.

~~cars~~   balloons   robot   presents   cards   cake

6	_cars_	1	_____	3	_____
4	_____	5	_____	1	_____

What Weather!

Lesson 1

1 Read and draw.

①
It's sunny.

②
It's rainy.

③
It's windy.

④
It's cloudy.

⑤
It's snowy.

⑥
It's stormy.

Vocabulary sunny, rainy, windy, cloudy, snowy, stormy

2 Lesson 2

1 Look, read, and write.

snowy ~~cloudy~~ rainy stormy windy sunny

What's the weather like?

①

It's _cloudy_ .

②

It's _____ .

③

It's _____ .

④

It's _____ .

⑤

It's _____ .

⑥

It's _____ .

1 | Read, circle, and write.

①

dry / (stormy)

It's _____ !

②

cold / dry

It's _____ !

③

rainy / sunny

It's _____ !

④

hot / snowy

It's _____ !

①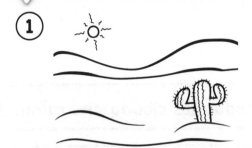

(It's dry.) / It's wet.

②

It's dry. / It's wet.

③

It's hot. / It's cold.

④

It's hot. / It's cold.

Everyday English!

3 Look, read, and write.

a e i o u

①

I d_o_n't __nderst__nd!

L__t's ch__ck.

②

How __ld are y__u?

I'm n__ne.

M__, too!

1 Read, look, and number.

① Today it's windy and stormy. ③ Today it's cloudy and rainy.

② Today it's hot and sunny. ④ Today it's cold and snowy.

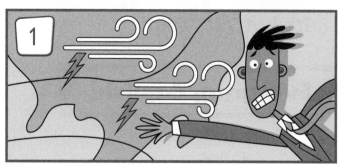

2 Draw the weather today. Read and write.

Today it's _____
and _____ .

1 Look, read, and make a ✓ or an ✗.

①

It's sunny. ☐

It's rainy. ☐

It's dry. ☐

②

It's snowy. ☐

It's rainy. ☐

It's windy. ☐

③

It's hot. ☐

It's cold. ☐

It's wet. ☐

2 Read and draw.

1 It's stormy and rainy.

2 It's cold and sunny.

Revision 1

1 Look, write, and match.

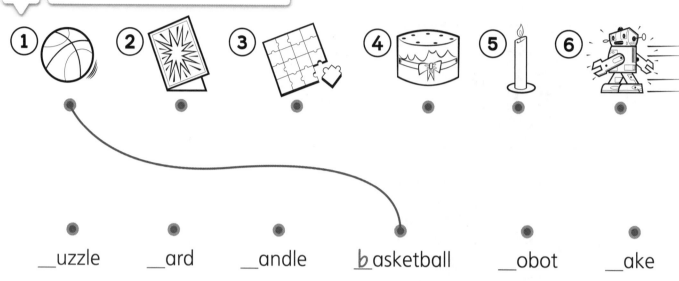

① ② ③ ④ ⑤ ⑥

__uzzle   __ard   __andle   <u>b</u> asketball   __obot   __ake

2 Look, read, and write.

stormy   snowy   ~~windy~~   cloudy   sunny   hot

3 Look, read, and count. Write.

presents ~~candle~~ balloons cakes cards clown

1 There's a ___candle___ .

2 There are nine _____ .

3 There's a _____ .

4 There are ten _____ .

5 There are two _____ .

6 There are two _____ .

4 Read, look, and number.

1 It's rainy.

2 It's wet.

3 It's windy.

4 It's dry.

5 It's cold.

6 It's hot.

My Clothes!

1 Read, find, and color.

1 gray socks   3 yellow hat   5 black boots

2 blue jacket   4 green pants   6 brown shoes

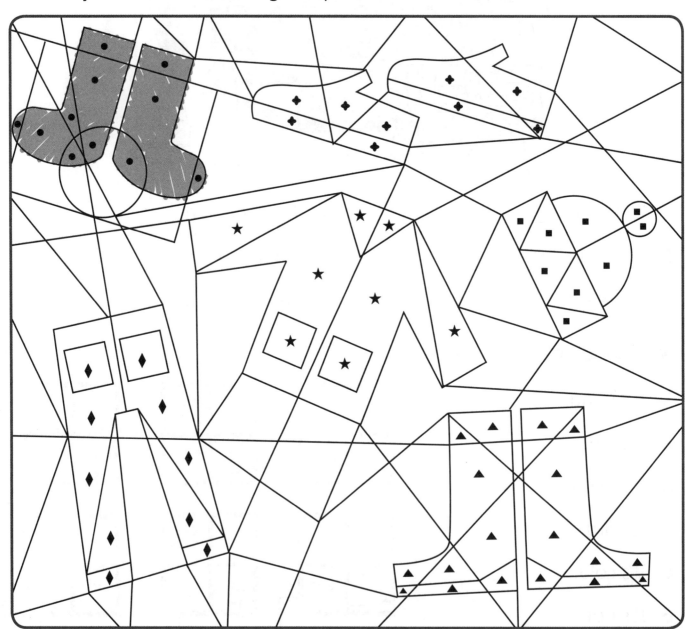

Vocabulary socks, jacket, hat, pants, boots, shoes

3 Lesson 2

1 Look, read, and circle.

①  It's windy.

Put on your hat!

~~Take off your hat!~~

②  It's wet.

Put on your boots!

Take off your boots!

③ 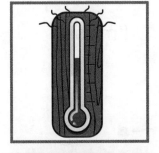 It's hot.

Put on your jacket!

Take off your jacket!

④  It's cold.

Put on your sweater!

Take off your sweater!

⑤  It's sunny.

Put on your hat!

Take off your hat!

1 Who's missing? Match. Then read and circle.

①

②

A skirt!

A sweater!

I'm hot.

I'm cold.

③

I'm hot.

~~I'm cold.~~

④

A T-shirt and shorts!

A T-shirt and a skirt!

2 Look, read, and match.

①

②

skirt   shorts   T-shirt   sweater

Everyday English!

3 Look, read, and write.

~~hat~~   jacket   T-shirt   Thanks   you

① How about a ___hat___ ?

② How about a _____ ?

Thank _____ !

③ How about a _____ ?

_____ !

1 Follow, read, and circle.

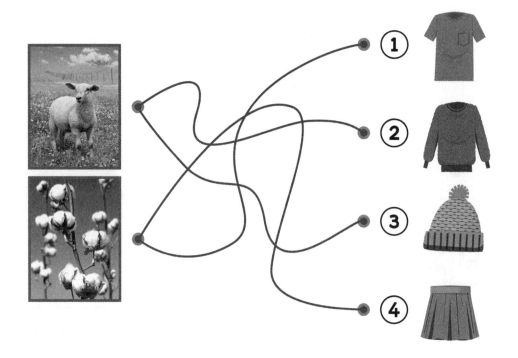

1. plant / sheep
   wool / cotton
2. (sheep) / plant
   cotton / (wool)
3. plant / sheep
   cotton / wool
4. sheep / plant
   wool / cotton

2 Look at some clothes. Draw.

cotton

wool

1 Look, read, and write.

Put on   Take off

①

___Put on___ your hat!

②

_____ your sweater!

③

_____ your jacket!

④

_____ your shoes!

⑤

_____ your boots!

⑥

_____ your T-shirt!

Home, Sweet Home

Lesson 1

1 Look, read, and write. Match.

a e i o

 (1)

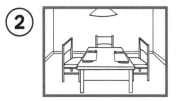 (2)

 (3)

 (4)

 (5)

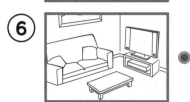 (6)

y _ rd

b _ dr _ _ m

l _ v _ ng r _ _m

k i tch e n

d _ n _ ng r _ _ m

b _ thr _ _ m

Vocabulary bedroom, bathroom, living room, dining room, kitchen, yard

1 Look and read. Write *He's* or *She's*. Then match.

① Where's Anna?

__She's__ in the ● ──────────────────── ● bedroom.

② Where's Grandpa?

_____ in the ● ● bathroom.

③ Where's Mom?

_____ in the ● ● living room.

④ Where's Grandma?

_____ in the ● ● kitchen.

⑤ Where's Dad?

_____ in the ● ● dining room.

1 Order the story. Choose and write.

bed   bathtub   sofa

Where's the _____ ?

1

Here's a _____ and a table!

Where's the _____ ?

2 Look, read, and number.

1 sofa

2 bed

3 table

4 bathtub

Everyday English!

3 Look, read, and write.   s w d k ~~h~~ t

How abou__ a hat?

Than__ you.

I'm __cared!

__on't __orry.

4 Lesson 4 | History

1 Look, read, and match.

2 Look, read, and write.

new   old

1 _____

2 _____

1 Look, read, and circle.

1 Where's the bathtub?   It's in the   bedroom.
~~dining room.~~

2 Where's the bed?   It's in the   yard.
living room.

3 Where's the sofa?   It's in the   kitchen.
bathroom.

4 Where's the table?   It's in the   kitchen.
living room.

Revision 2

1 Find, circle, and write.

n	f	s	p	a	p	t	d
b	y	w	m	n	a	s	r
s	i	e	g	o	n	a	j
l	b	a	t	h	t	u	b
e	t	t	o	w	s	u	w
b	u	e	r	s	y	c	a
o	q	r	k	o	p	e	l
o	e	t	z	f	m	s	o
t	x	i	t	a	b	l	e
s	n	a	v	h	g	c	r

① 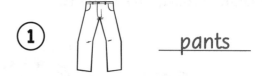 _pants_

②  _____

③  _____

④  _____

⑤  _____

⑥  _____

2 Look, write, and match.

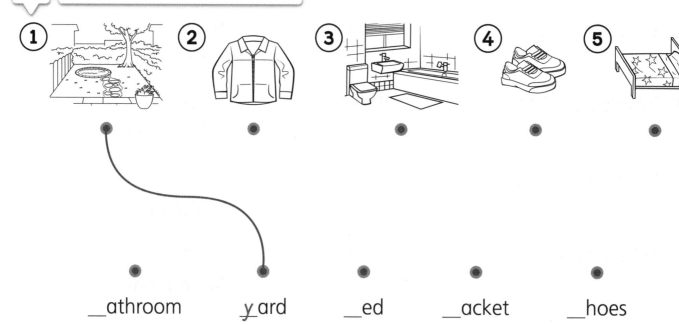

① ② ③ ④ ⑤

__athroom   _y_ard   __ed   __acket   __hoes

3 Look, read, and number.

①  ②  ③  ④

Take off your shorts. ☐   Take off your socks. ☐

Put on your shoes. ☐   Put on your skirt. 1

4 Find, read, and write.

living room   yard   ~~bedroom~~   kitchen

①  It's in the _bedroom_ .   ②  It's in the _____ .

③ It's in the _____ .   ④ It's in the _____ .

At the Beach

1 Look, read, and write.

swim   climb   run   ~~sing~~   dive   cook

①

_____sing_____

②

_____

③

_____

④

_____

⑤

_____

⑥

_____

5 Lesson 2

1 Read, look, and number.

① I can dive.

② I can cook.

③ I can swim.

④ I can climb.

⑤ I can't dive.

⑥ I can't cook.

⑦ I can't swim.

⑧ I can't climb.

1 Read, circle, and write.

①

swim / dance / cook

I can _____ !

②

climb / swim / jump

I can _____ !

③

climb / catch / dive

I can _____ !

④

dance / fly / sing

I can't _____ !

2 Look, match, and write.

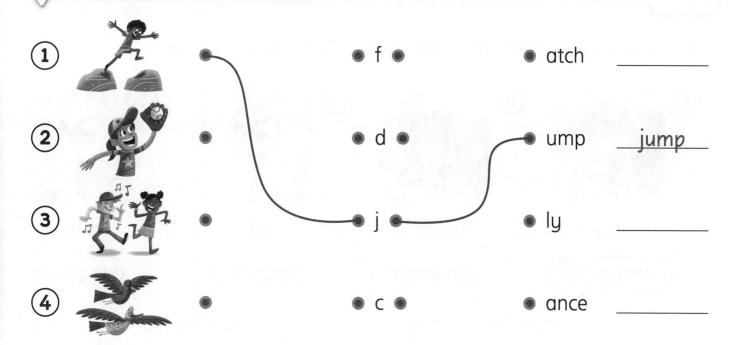

1. f • atch _____

2. d • ump ___jump___

3. j • ly _____

4. c • ance _____

Everyday English!

3 Look, read, and match.

1.
   • Oh, no!

   • Quick!

2.
   • I don't understand.

   • Let's check.

1 Look, read, and circle. Color the flags green or red.

①
safe
~~dangerous~~ (circled)

②
safe
dangerous

③
safe
dangerous

④
safe
dangerous

safe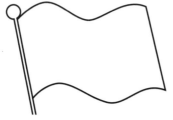

dangerous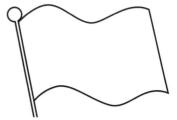

2 Look, read, and write.

safe   dangerous

1 <u>dangerous</u>

2 _____

3 _____

4 _____

5 Review

1 Write *can* or *can't* for you. Look and match.

1 I ____can____ swim.

2 I _____ jump.

3 I _____ dance.

4 I _____ run.

5 I _____ fly.

6 I _____ sing.

6 Animal Fun!

Lesson 1

1 Find, circle, and match.

1

2

3

goatpigchickenhorseduckcow

4

5

6

Vocabulary goat, pig, chicken, horse, duck, cow

1 Read and match. Write *Yes, it can.* or *No, it can't.*

1 Can a horse jump?

Can it fly?

2 Can a pig sing?

Can it run?

3 Can a goat climb?

Can it dance?

4 Can a bird cook?

Can it fly?

Yes, it can.

No, it can't.

5 Can a duck swim?

Can it jump?

Grammar Can a horse jump? Can it fly? Yes, it can. No, it can't.

1 Read, choose, and write.

bat   fox   ~~squirrel~~   frog

① squirrel

② _____

③ _____

④ _____

2 **Look, read, and color. Write.**

①

___squirrel___

A green frog.

A brown fox.

A gray squirrel.

A black bat.

②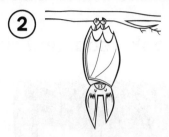

_____

③

_____

④

_____

Everyday English!

3 **Look, read, and write. Draw.**

~~animal~~   scared   squirrel   favorite   worry

What's your favorite ___animal___ ?

A bat!

I'm _____ !

Don't _____ . What's your _____ animal?

A _____ !

6 Lesson 4 | Science

1 Look, read, and circle.

It's (day) / night time.

It's awake /(asleep).

It's **day** / night time.

It's awake / asleep.

It's **day** / night time.

It's awake / asleep.

It's **day** / night time.

It's awake / asleep.

2 Read and draw. Write.

night awake day asleep

It's _____ time. I'm _____ .

It's _____ time. I'm _____ .

Vocabulary night time, day time, awake, asleep

6 Review

1 Read, write, and circle.

bird   goat   ~~fox~~   frog   squirrel   bat

①

Can a ___fox___ fly?

Yes, it can. / (No, it can't.)

②

Can a _____ jump?

Yes, it can. / No, it can't.

③

Can a _____ climb?

Yes, it can. / No, it can't.

④

Can a _____ run?

Yes, it can. / No, it can't.

⑤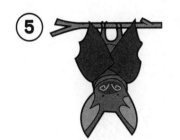

Can a _____ fly?

Yes, it can. / No, it can't.

⑥

Can a _____ sing?

Yes, it can. / No, it can't.

Revision 3

1 Unscramble and write.

①  xfo

②  rofg

③ odg

④ otag

___fox___ _____ _____ _____

2 Look, read, and write. Find the mystery animal.

duck ~~climb~~ dance cow dive squirrel catch

①

②

③

④

⑤

⑥

⑦

		¹c	l	i	m	b
2						
	3					
		4				
5						
6						
	7					

The mystery animal is a c _ _ _ _ _ _ _ .

3 Look, read, and write.

| can   can   ~~can't~~   can't | swim   dive   ~~cook~~   climb |

① I <u>can't cook</u> .

② I _____ .

③ I _____ .

④ I _____ .

4 Look, read, and match.

1 Can it jump? ●
2 Can it fly? ●
3 Can it run? ●

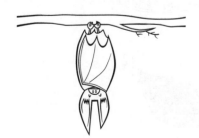

4 Can it dive? ●
5 Can it run? ●
6 Can it fly? ●

● Yes, it can.

● No, it can't.

Picnic Time!

1 What's next? Look, read, and write.

rice   chicken   pasta   ~~salad~~   cheese   milk

①   _salad_

②    _____

③   _____

④       _____

⑤   _____

⑥   _____

Vocabulary rice, chicken, pasta, salad, cheese, milk

7 Lesson 2

1 Read and draw ☺ or ☹. Write *like* or *don't like*.

I like milk.
I like pasta.
I don't like chicken.
I like rice.
I don't like cheese.
I like salad.

①

☺

I ___like___ pasta.

②

😐

I _____ salad.

③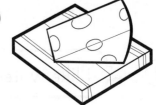

😐

I _____ cheese.

④

😐

I _____ chicken.

⑤

😐

I _____ milk.

⑥

😐

I _____ rice.

1 Look, read, and match. Write.

(1) I like candy.

I like _____ .

(2) I like water.

I like _____ .

(3) I like fries.

I like _candy_ .

(4) I like ice cream.

I like _____ .

2 Look, read, and unscramble. Match.

water ~~ice cream~~ candy fries

① I like cei ramec .

② I like dyanc .

③ I like twera .

④ I like sferi .

ice cream

Everyday English!

3 Look, read, and number.

① I feel sick.

② What's wrong?

③ Thank you!

④ Quick! Water.

1 Look and number in order. Read and write.

Where does cheese come from?

c l g k r ~~c~~ w ~~h~~ ~~s~~ m t

<u>c</u> <u>h</u> ee <u>s</u> e s __ ore

__ i __ __

__ o __   __ __ ass

2 Look, read, and write.   grass   store

①

②

_____   _____

1 Follow, write, and draw ☺ or ☹.

candy   ice cream   fries   cheese   ~~pasta~~   milk

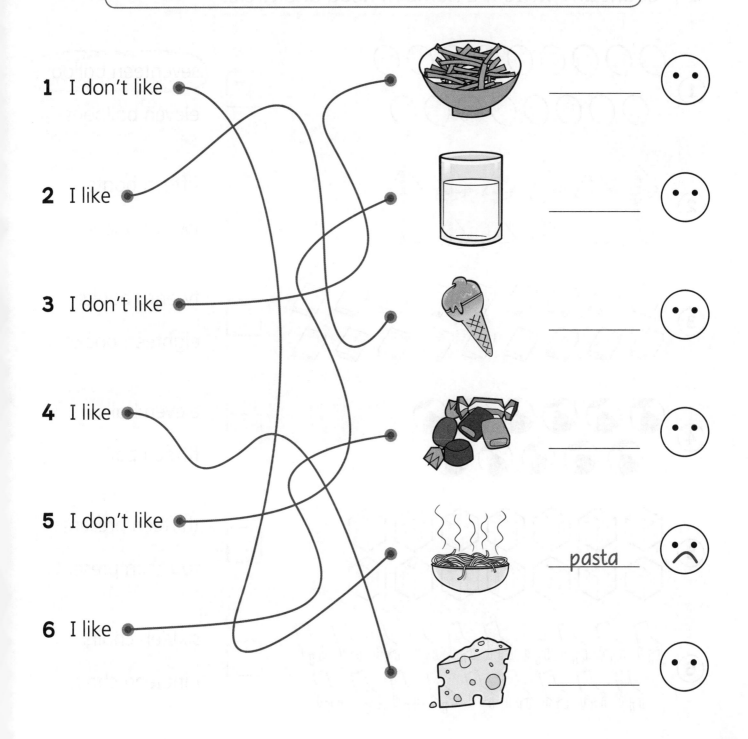

1 I don't like

2 I like

3 I don't like

4 I like

5 I don't like

6 I like

pasta

Numbers Everywhere!

Lesson 1

1 | Count and write the number. Read and circle.

1 17 — (seventeen balloons)
eleven balloons

2 ☐ fifteen boats
twelve boats

3 ☐ twenty books
eighteen books

4 ☐ eleven balls
fifteen balls

5 ☐ thirteen presents
fourteen presents

6 ☐ sixteen chairs
nineteen chairs

1 | Count and write the number. Write *have* or *don't have*.

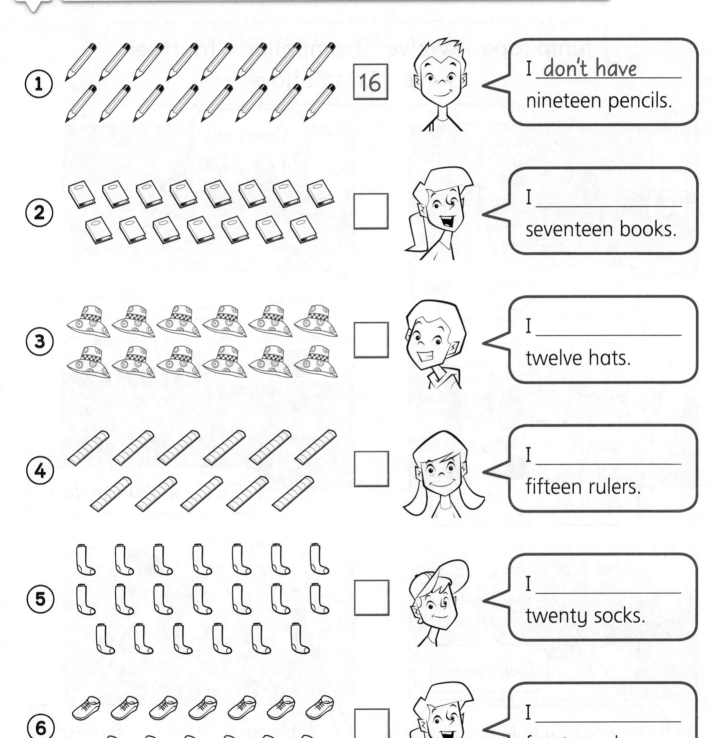

① 16 I _don't have_ nineteen pencils.

② I _____ seventeen books.

③ I _____ twelve hats.

④ I _____ fifteen rulers.

⑤ I _____ twenty socks.

⑥ I _____ fourteen shoes.

Grammar I have sixteen pencils. I don't have nineteen pencils.

1 Order the story. Choose and write.

jump rope   twelve   trampoline   fourteen
I have   I don't have

Eleven?   Wow, Ellie!

Come on!

Thirteen, _____ , fifteen!

Look! It's Sports Day.

1

Cool! A _____ !

Go, Lucy! You can do it!

Don't worry!

_____ a hula hoop
and a _____ , but ...

Jump on!

Eleven, _____ , thirteen!

Oh no! _____ a skateboard!

2 Follow, read, and write.

jump rope   hula hoop   trampoline   ~~skateboard~~

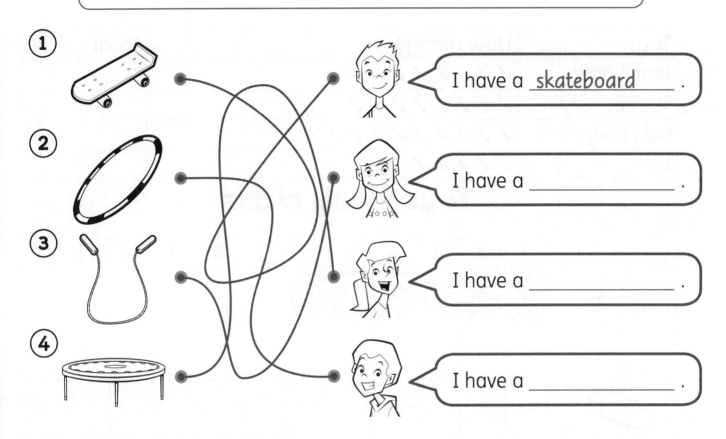

① I have a _skateboard_ .

② I have a _____ .

③ I have a _____ .

④ I have a _____ .

Everyday English!

3 Look, read, and number.

① I'm scared!

② Don't worry. You can do it!

③ What's wrong?

1 Count and write the numbers. Color the blocks.

Toys	How many?	Total
skateboard	✓ ✓ ✓ ✓ ✓ ✓	6
scooter	✓ ✓ ✓ ✓ ✓ ✓ ✓	
hula hoop	✓ ✓ ✓ ✓ ✓ ✓ ✓ ✓ ✓ ✓	
kite	✓ ✓ ✓ ✓ ✓	

Toys in my class

	1	2	3	4	5	6	7	8	9	10	11	12
skateboard	■	■	■	■	■	■						
scooter												
hula hoop												
kite												

2 Look, read, and match.

①
Kim

I have a jump rope and two skateboards. I don't have a kite.

②
Dan

I have three kites and two jump ropes. I don't have a skateboard.

	Dan	Kim
jump rope	1	2
skateboard	2	–
kite	–	3

1 Match and write.

14

13

18

11

17

- s __ __ entee __
- __ leve __
- __ __ irt __ __ n
- f our t een
- eight __ __ __

2 Look, read, and number.

① I don't have a jump rope.
I have a trampoline.

② I have a skateboard.
I don't have a hula hoop.

③ I have a hula hoop.
I don't have a trampoline.

④ I don't have a skateboard.
I have a jump rope.

  ☐ 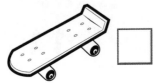 ☐  1  ☐

Revision 4

1 Look, match, and write.

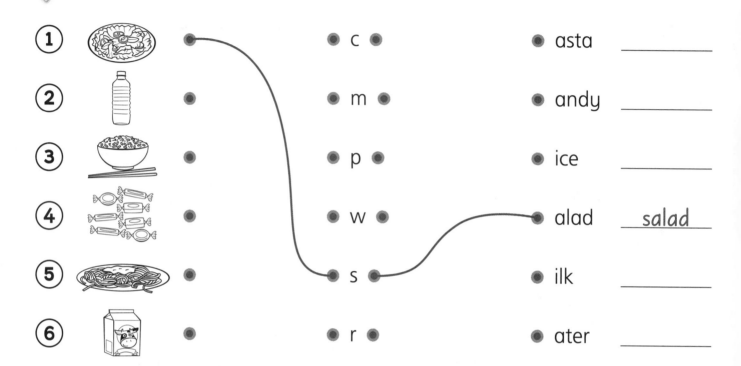

1.   • c •   • asta   _____
2.   • m •   • andy   _____
3.   • p •   • ice   _____
4.   • w •   • alad   _salad_
5.   • s •   • ilk   _____
6.   • r •   • ater   _____

2 Find, circle, and match. Write.

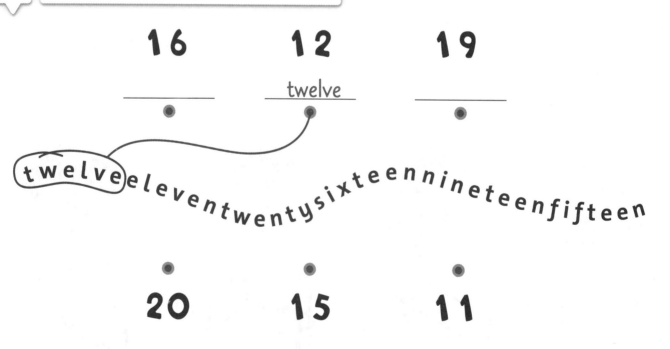

16   12   19

_____   _twelve_   _____

t w e l v e e l e v e n t w e n t y s i x t e e n n i n e t e e n f i f t e e n

20   15   11

_____   _____   _____

3 Look and write *like* or *don't like*.

I ___don't like___ cheese. I _____ rice.

I _____ salad. I _____ chicken.

I _____ fries. I _____ ice cream.

4 Look, read, and make a ✓ or an ✗.

I have a chicken.
I don't have a duck.
I don't have a trampoline.
I have a skateboard.
I have a T-shirt.
I don't have a sweater.

1 Write the words. Find and number.

■	❀	◎	✸	✧	▲	◗	➤	▣	◆	✳	✳	○
a	b	c	d	e	f	g	h	i	j	k	l	m

✛	☆	⬢	▢	✴	⊙	✧	♥	◈	●	▲	❊	★
n	o	p	q	r	s	t	u	v	w	x	y	z

① ⬢ ✴ ✧ ⊙ ✧ ✛ ✧

<u>p</u> <u>r</u> <u>e</u> <u>s</u> <u>e</u> <u>n</u> <u>t</u>

② ▲ ✳ ☆ ● ✧ ✴ ⊙

_ _ _ _ _ _ _

③ ➤ ♥ ◗

_ _ _

④ ❀ ✴ ✧ ■ ✳ ▲ ■ ⊙ ✧

_ _ _ _ _ _ _ _ _

⑤ ◎ ■ ✴ ✸

_ _ _ _

⑥ ◎ ☆ ☆ ✳ ▣ ✧ ⊙

_ _ _ _ _ _ _

Vocabulary hug, cookies, flowers, breakfast

2 Design a Mother's Day breakfast. Draw or write.

Halloween

1 Look, read, and write.

> pumpkin ghost cake candle
> skeleton balloons ~~cat~~ mask

Vocabulary skeleton, ghost, mask, pumpkin

2 Design two pumpkin faces. Draw and color.

OXFORD
UNIVERSITY PRESS

Great Clarendon Street, Oxford, OX2 6DP, United Kingdom

Oxford University Press is a department of the University of Oxford.
It furthers the University's objective of excellence in research, scholarship,
and education by publishing worldwide. Oxford is a registered trade
mark of Oxford University Press in the UK and in certain other countries

ISBN: 978 0 19 403364 0

Printed in China

This book is printed on paper from certified and well-managed sources

ACKNOWLEDGEMENTS

Back cover photograph: Oxford University Press building/David Fisher

Cover Image: Linda Cavallini/Advocate Art.

Illustrations by: Linda Cavallini/Advocate Art p.3, 6, 12, 20, 26, 31 (house), 34, 40,
48, 54; Luke Flowers/The Bright Agency p.35 (actions); Andy Hamilton pp.11,
13, 16 (climate symbols), 17 (party scene), 19, 24, 25, 30, 38, 39, 41 (animals),
43 (bird and goat), 44 (actions), 45 (animals), 46, 49 (food), 51 (milk, ice cream
and pasta), 53 (hats, socks and shoes), 55 (trampoline), 58, 59 (ice cream, fries,
chicken, duck, trampoline, skateboard, T-shirt and jumper), 62; John Haslam
pp.8, 9, 14, 15, 21, 27, 29, 33, 36 (beach scene), 41 (girl and boy), 43 (fox, frog,
bat and squirrel), 45 (characters), 49 (boy and girl), 50 (countryside), 51 (fries,
candy and cheese), 55 (children climbing), 63; Andrew Painter pp.2, 4, 5, 7,
8 (half car and house), 13 (children in classroom), 16 (objects), 17, 18, 21 (boy
in sunhat and girl with scarf), 23, 28, 31 (children), 32, 35 (children on the
beach), 36 (flag), 37, 42, 44 (animals), 47, 50 (road with houses), 52, 53 (pencils,
books, rulers and children), 55 (skateboard, hula hoop, skipping rope and
children), 56 (children), 57, 59 (rice, chicken, salad, cheese and boys); Mark
Ruffle pp.22, 36 (lifeguard tower and sign).

*The publishers would like to thank the following for permission to reproduce photographs
and other copyright material*: Alamy p.60 (breakfast in bed/© Blend Images);
Corbis pp.49 (Hispanic boy/Blend Images/Inti St Clair, white boy/PhotoAlto/
Odilon Dimier, blonde girl/John Smith); 60 (girl icing biscuits/Blend Images/
Ariel Skelley); Oxford University Press p.49 african girl/Photoconcepts;
Shutterstock pp.22 (sheep/Elena Elisseeva, cotton plant/Moises Fernandez
Acosta), 28 (old chair/Stacy Barnett, new sofa/abramsdesign, new bath/risteski
goce, new chair/Just2shutter, old sofa/Mike Stone, old bath/Ttatty), 50 (cow/
smereka, cheese on sale/Adisa, curd cheese/Olaf Speier, heated milk/Olaf
Speier, cows being milked/Sukpaiboonwat), 60 (hug/Monkey Business Images,
present/Snvv, card/Mega Pixel).